Errata

Dan Locklair

FANTASY BRINGS THE DAY

for harpsichord

Page 3 (first page of music), system # 6:

       The final 8 notes of this system (now sixteenth notes)
       <u>should all be thirty-second notes.</u>

Page 5, system #6:

       The 8 notes that make up the fourth grouping of scalar
       pitches in this system (now sixteenth notes)
       <u>should all be thirty-second notes.</u>

       [N.B. The 3 sixteenth note chords that follow the above notes are
       correct.]

e.c. kerby, ltd. (Ricordi)
music publishers

[Distributed by Hal Leonard]

Dan Locklair

FANTASY BRINGS THE DAY

for harpsichord

To and for Barbara Harbach

e.c. kerby ltd.

Distributed by

Hal Leonard Publishing Corporation

7777 West Bluemound Road   P.O. Box 13819   Milwaukee, Wisconsin 53213

Fantasy Brings the Day

(for harpsichord)

Section I

Dan Locklair

II (top) 8'
I (bottom) 8' 4'
Manuals coupled

* **N.B.** Please note that the key signature of Sections I and II is F♯ and G♯ only.
  All C's are ♮ unless otherwise noted.

** 𝟎 = Free meter, quarter note
  equals the beat.

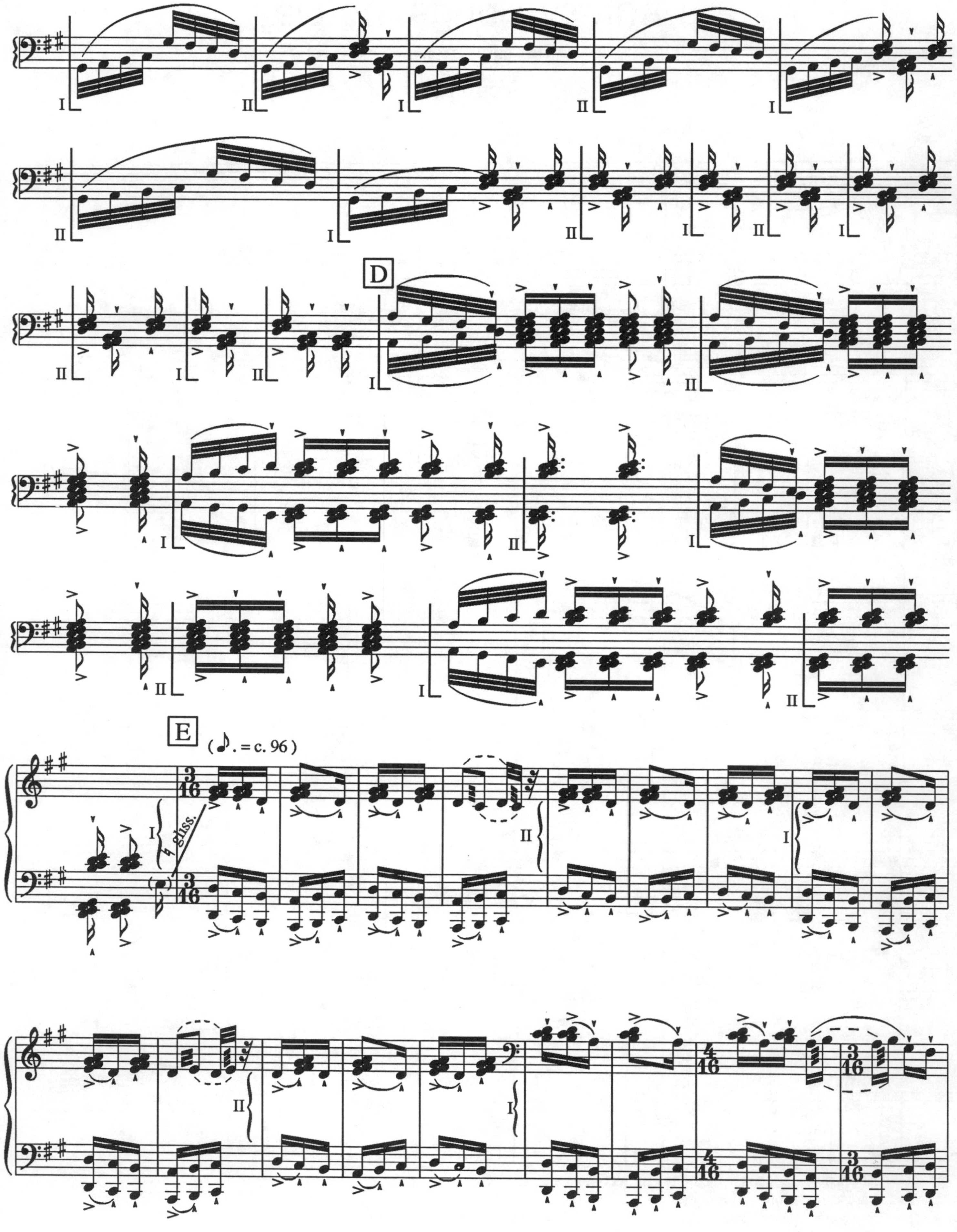
D
E
(♪. = c. 96)
gliss.

F As before (♩ = c. 100)

6

Broaden (greatly) - - - ♩ = c. 60

Slowing - - -

short

[uncouple manuals]

short

Attacca

Reflective (♩ = c. 60) (♪ = ♪)   Section II

- 4' on I while playing

H Same tempo (♩ = c. 60)
(very expressive, flexible and watery)

I

* Hold all pitches with L.V. indications (⌣)
   until either: 1) A comma (') appears
                  2) The note is repeated
                  3) A ⌢ ƒ appears

* ' = gentle lift of all held notes.

Duration: Section I = ca. 2' 30"; Section II = ca. 3' 30"; Section III = ca. 4' 30"; Section IV = ca. 2' 30"
Total duration = ca. 13 min.

Spring and summer 1989
Winston-Salem and Brevard,
North Carolina